The Alphabet

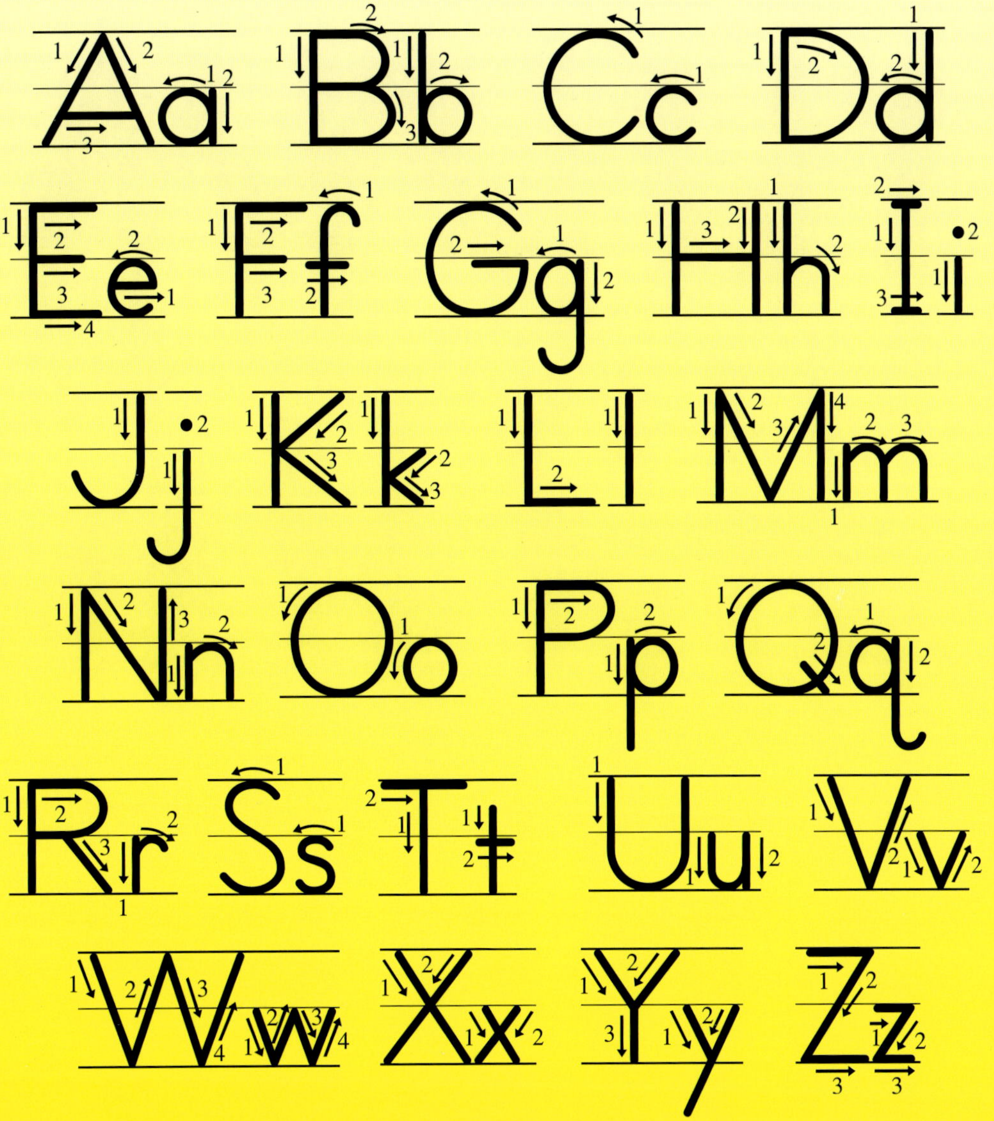

The Letter "A"

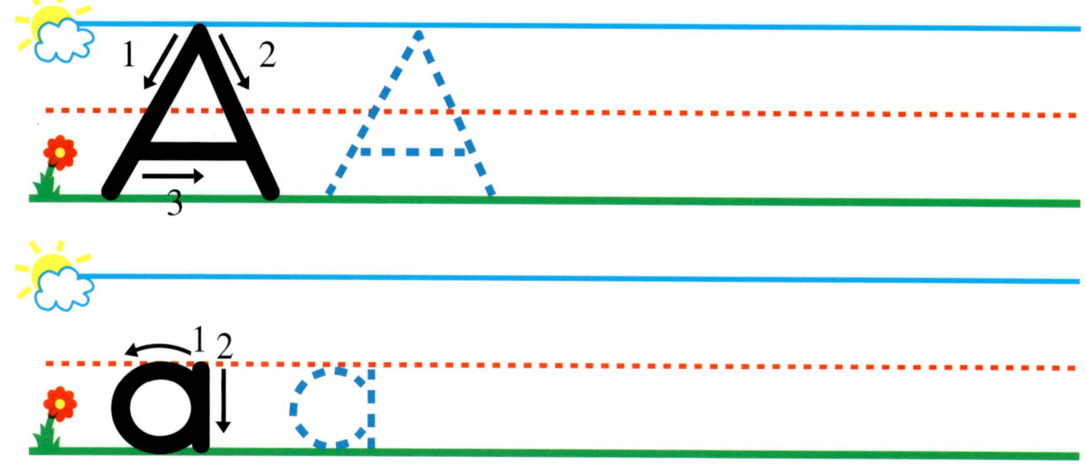

A is for apple.

The Letter "B"

B is for ball.

The Letter "C"

C is for corn.

The Letter "D"

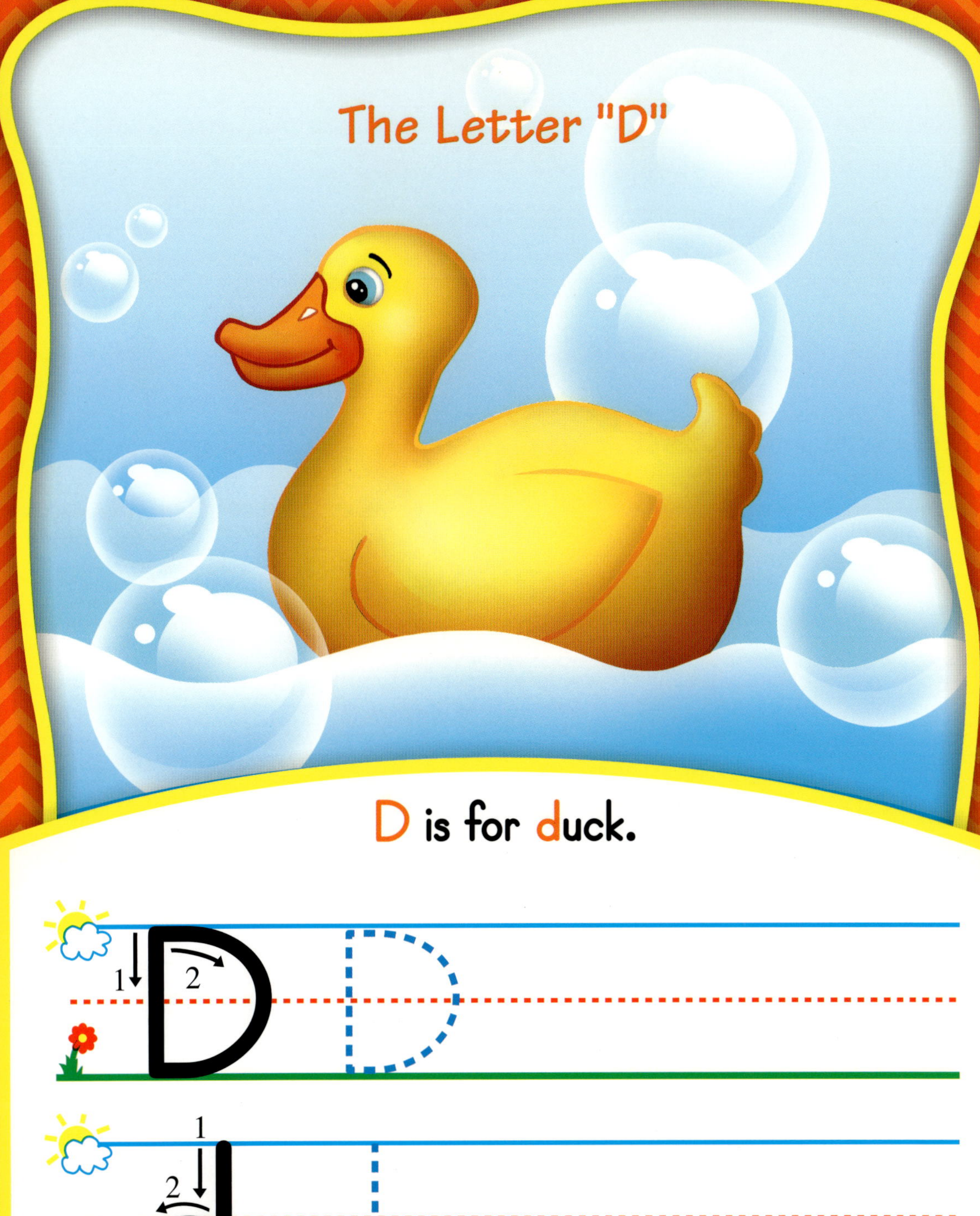

D is for duck.

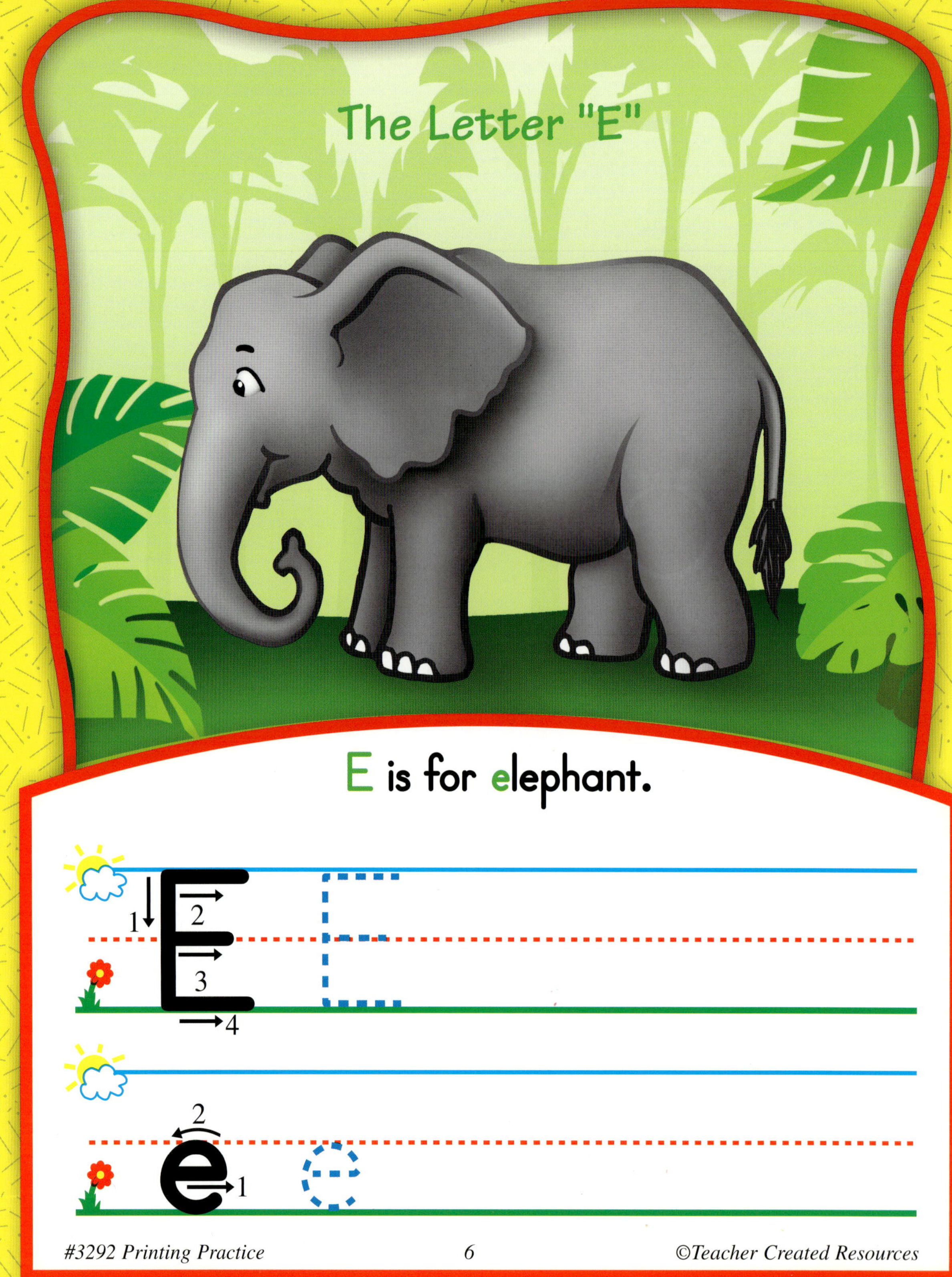

The Letter "E"
E is for elephant.
1 2 3 4
2 1

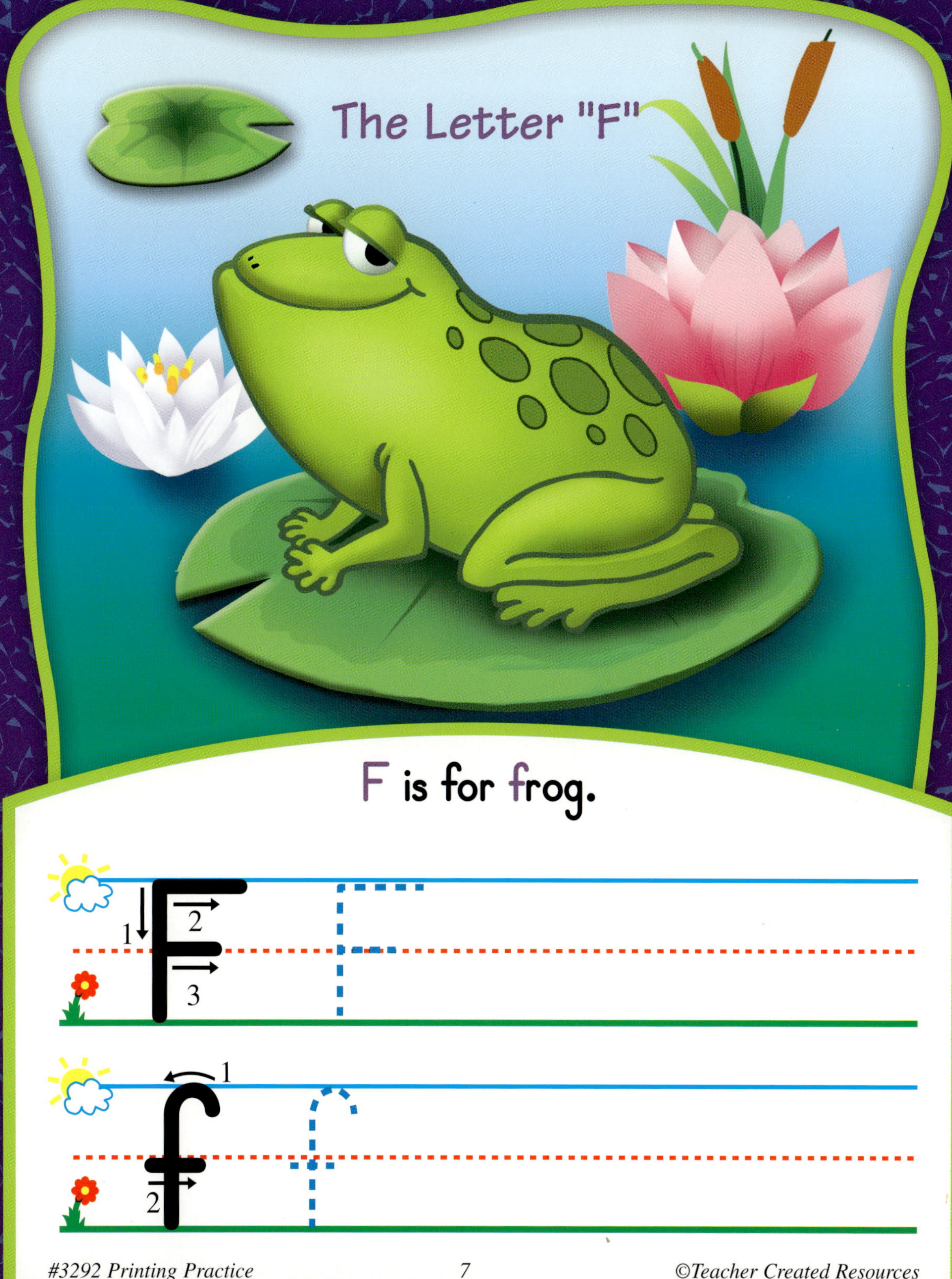

The Letter "F"
F is for frog.

The Letter "G"

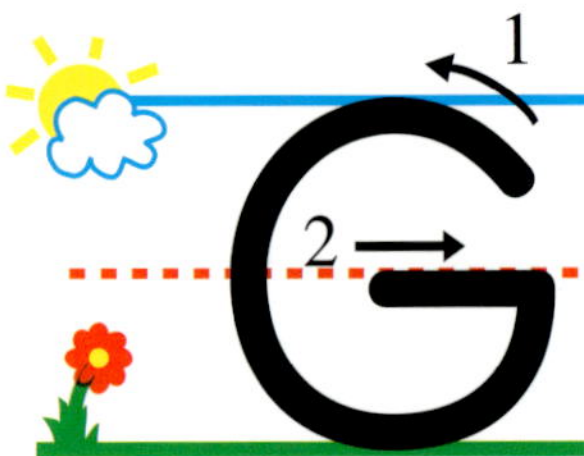

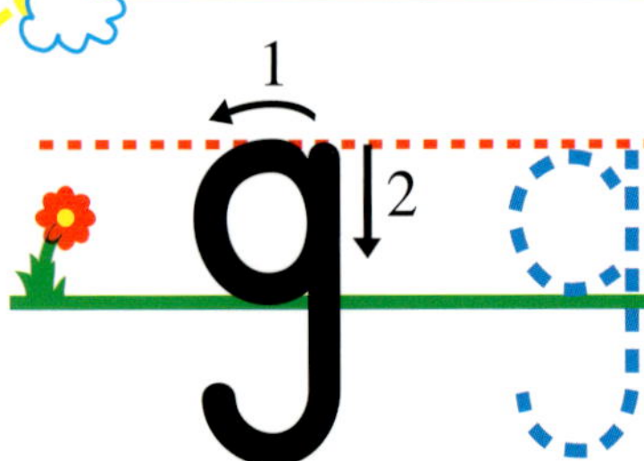

The Letter "H"

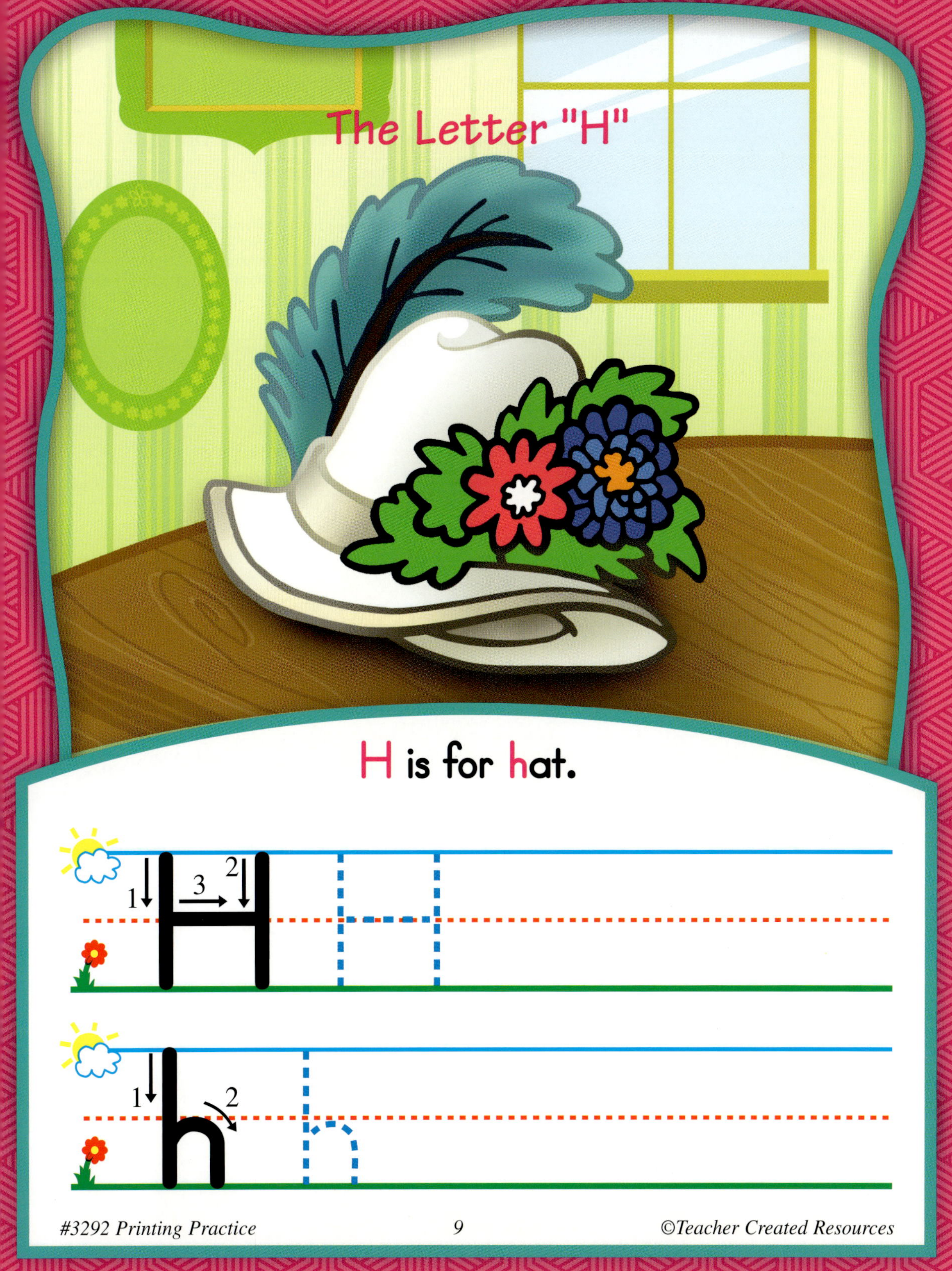

H is for **h**at.

The Letter "I"

I is for ice cream.

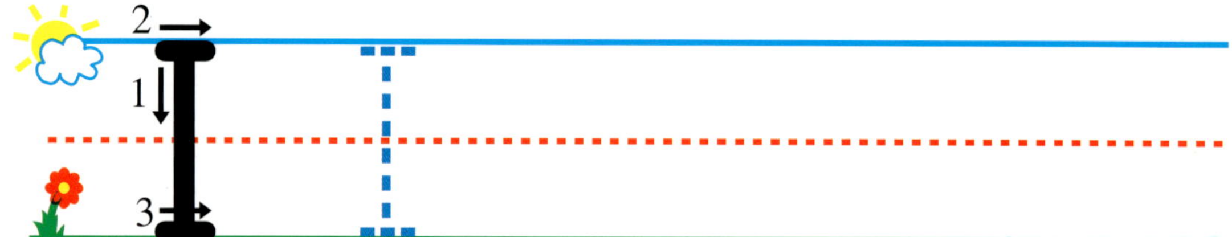

The Letter "J"

J is for jam.

The Letter "K"

K is for kite.

The Letter "L"

L is for lion.

The Letter "M"

M is for mouse.

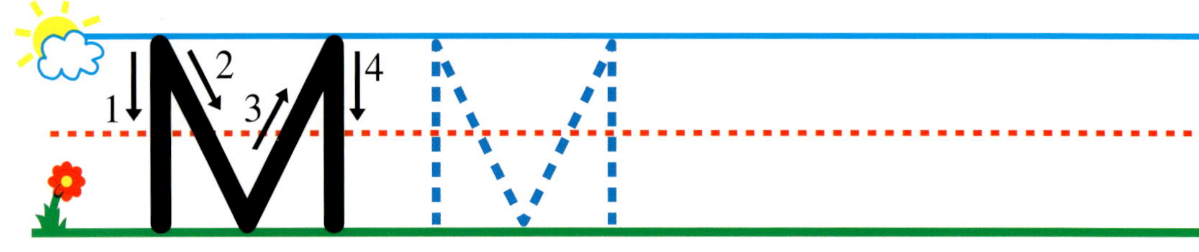

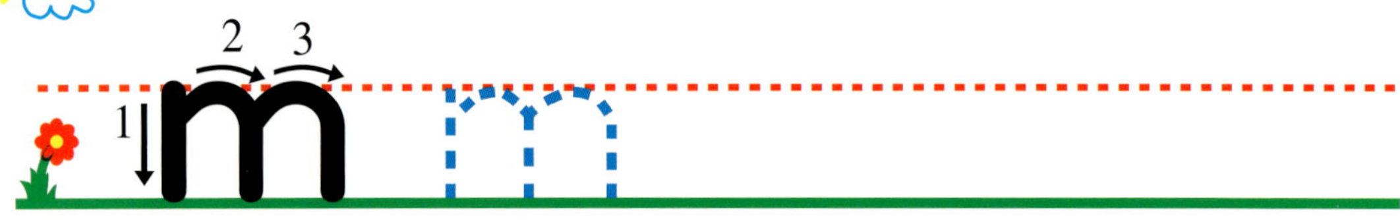

The Letter "N"

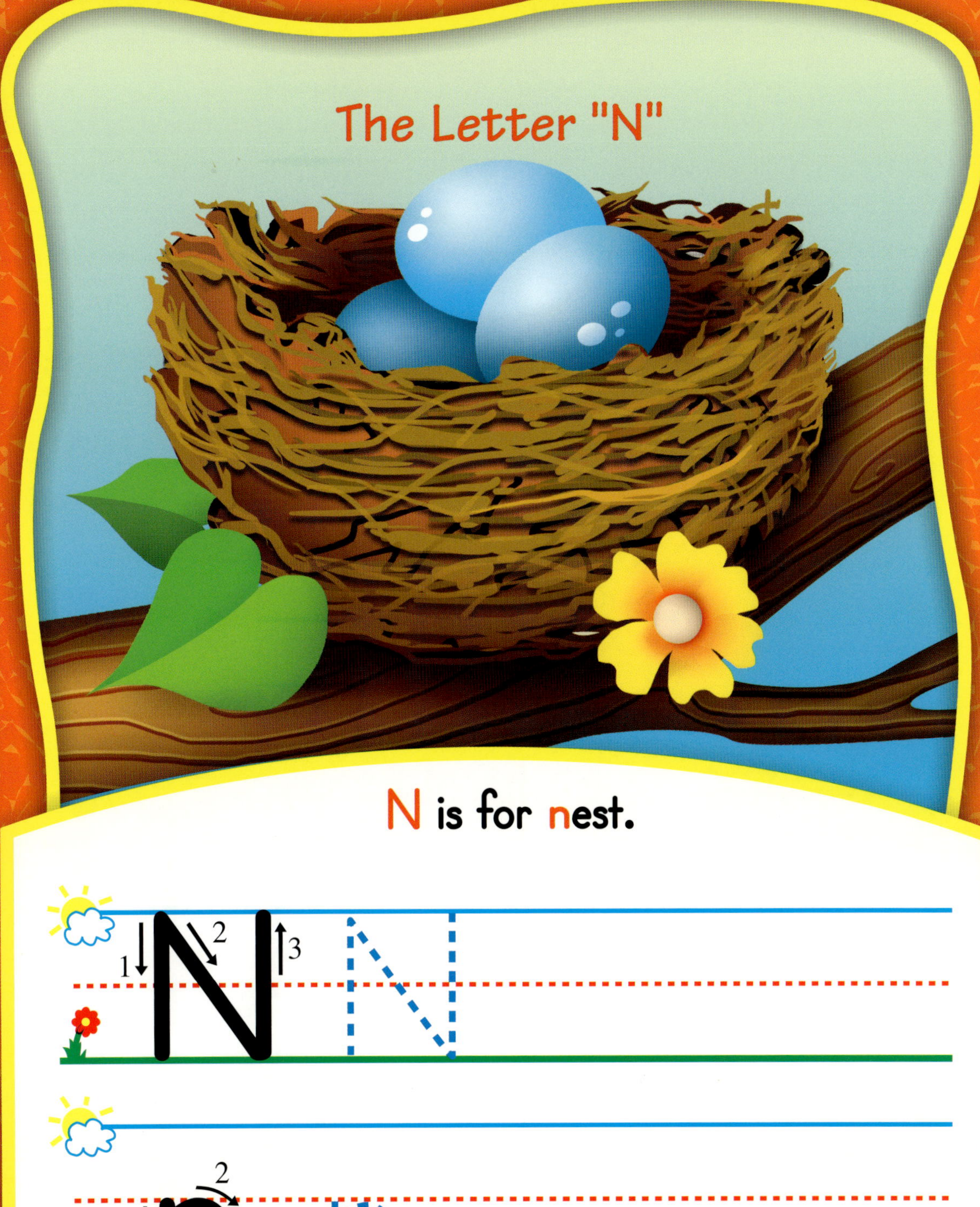

The Letter "O"

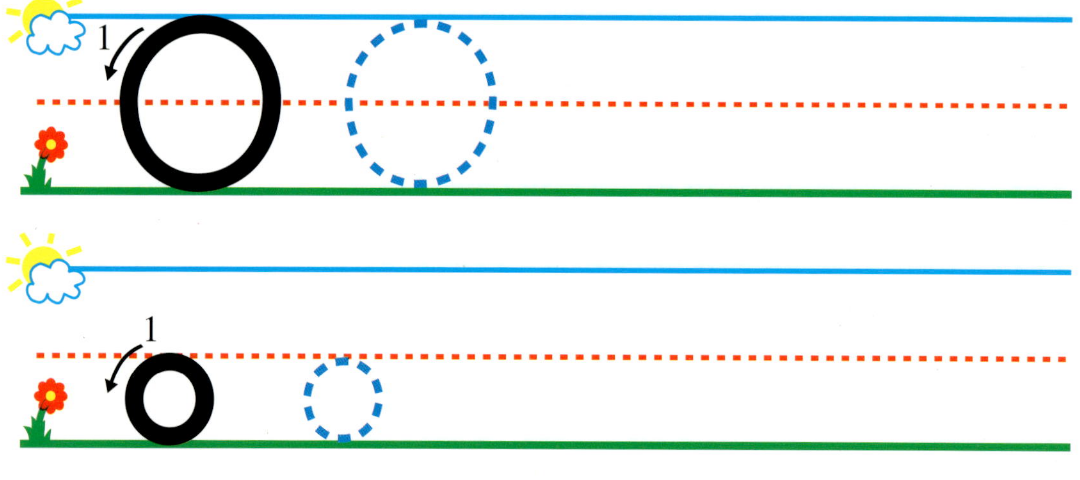

O is for **octopus**.

The Letter "P"

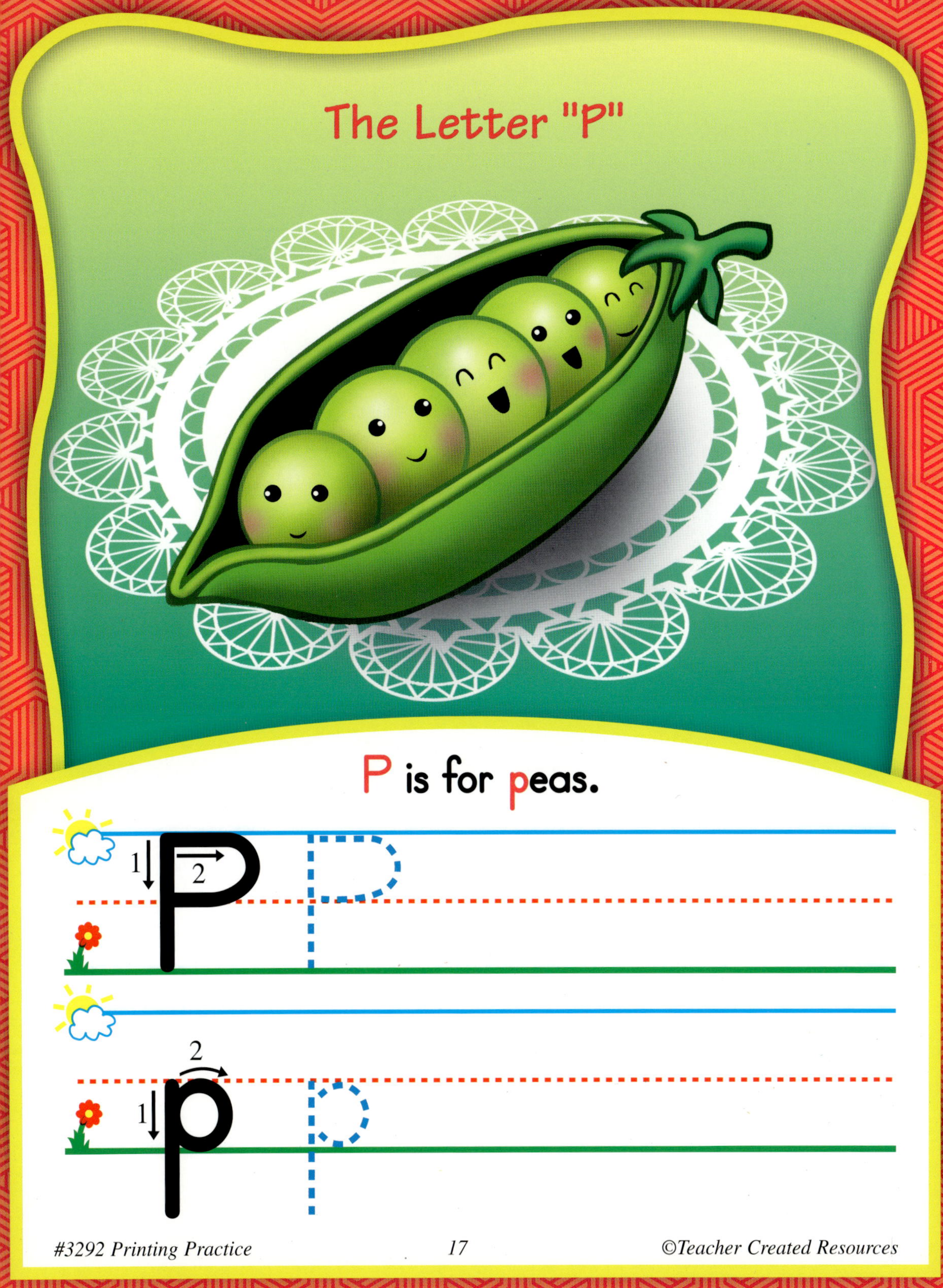

P is for **p**eas.

The Letter "Q"

Q is for queen.

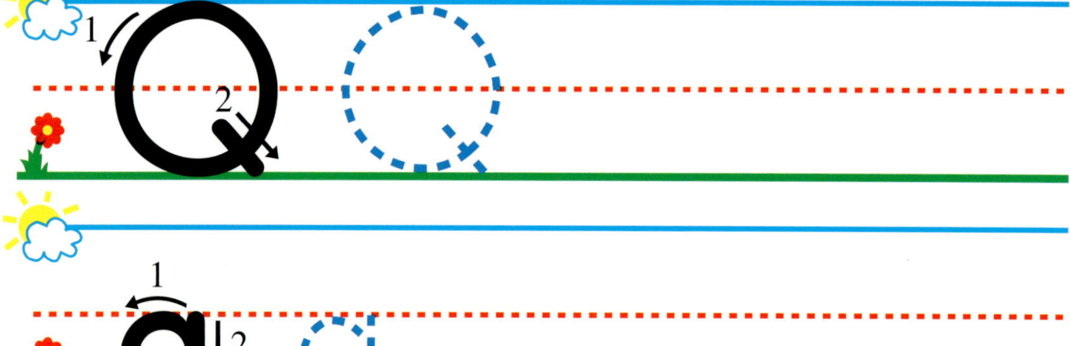

The Letter "R"

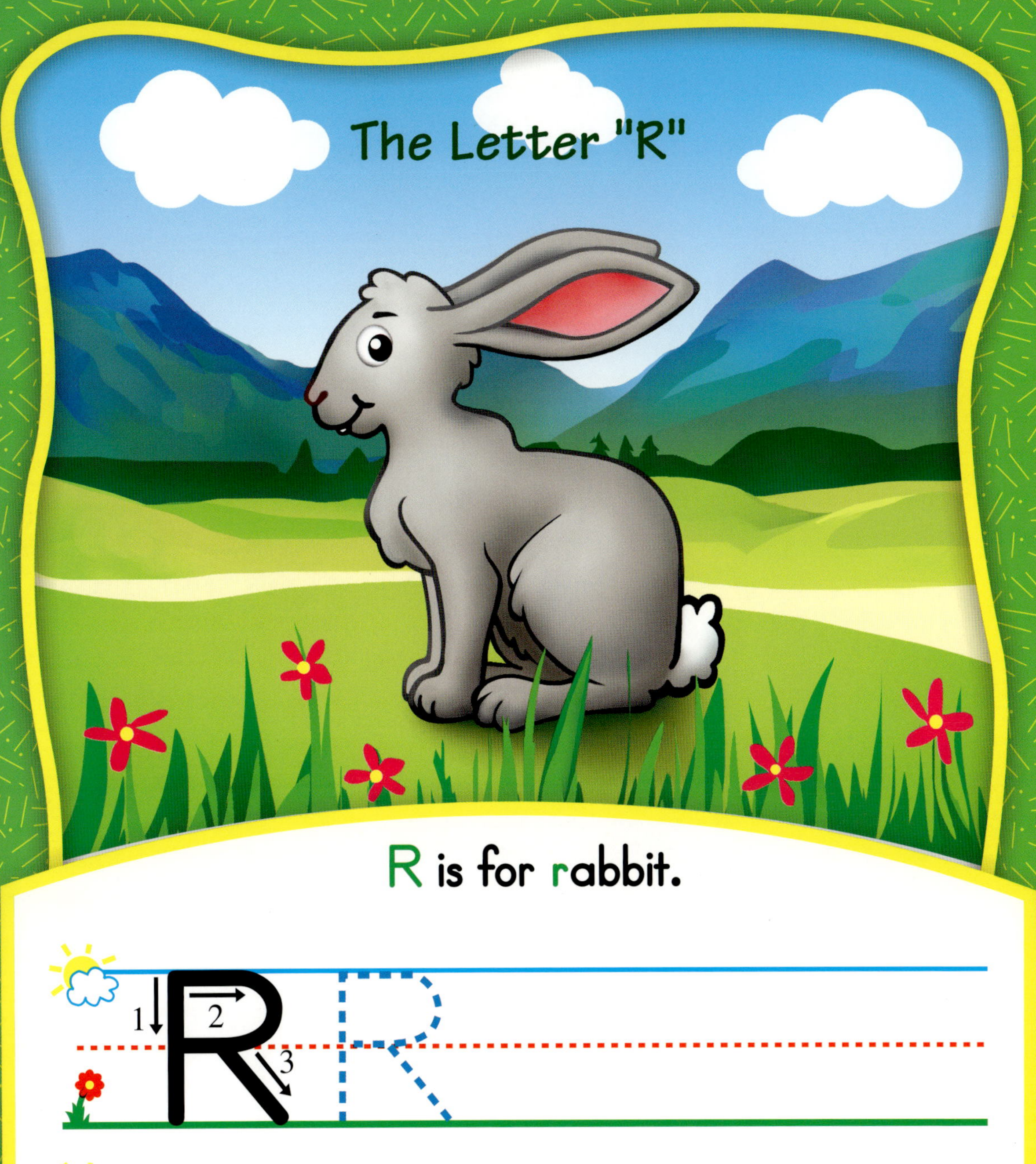

R is for rabbit.

The Letter "S"

S is for **sun**.

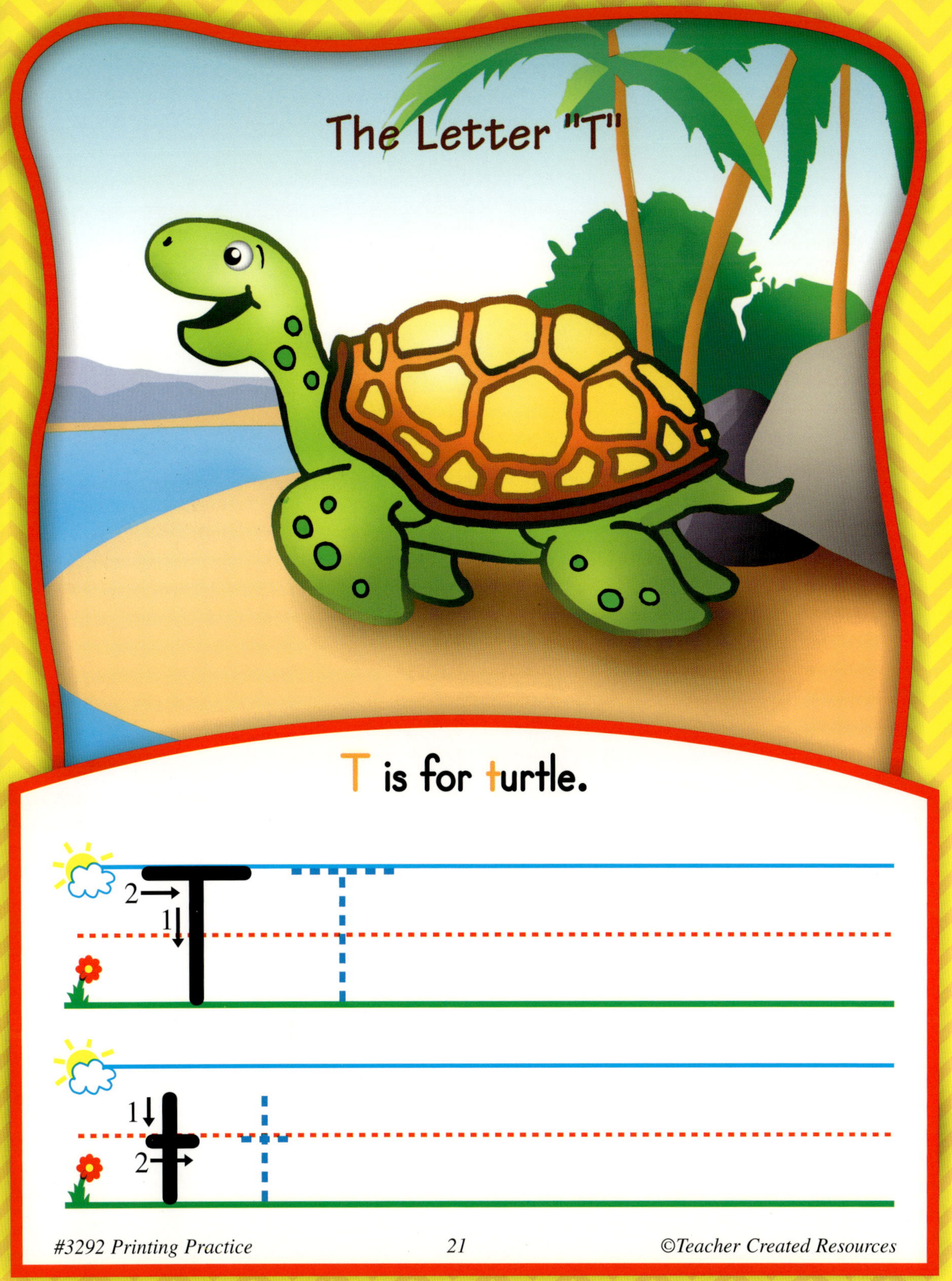

The Letter "T"

T is for turtle.

The Letter "U"

U is for umbrella.

The Letter "V"

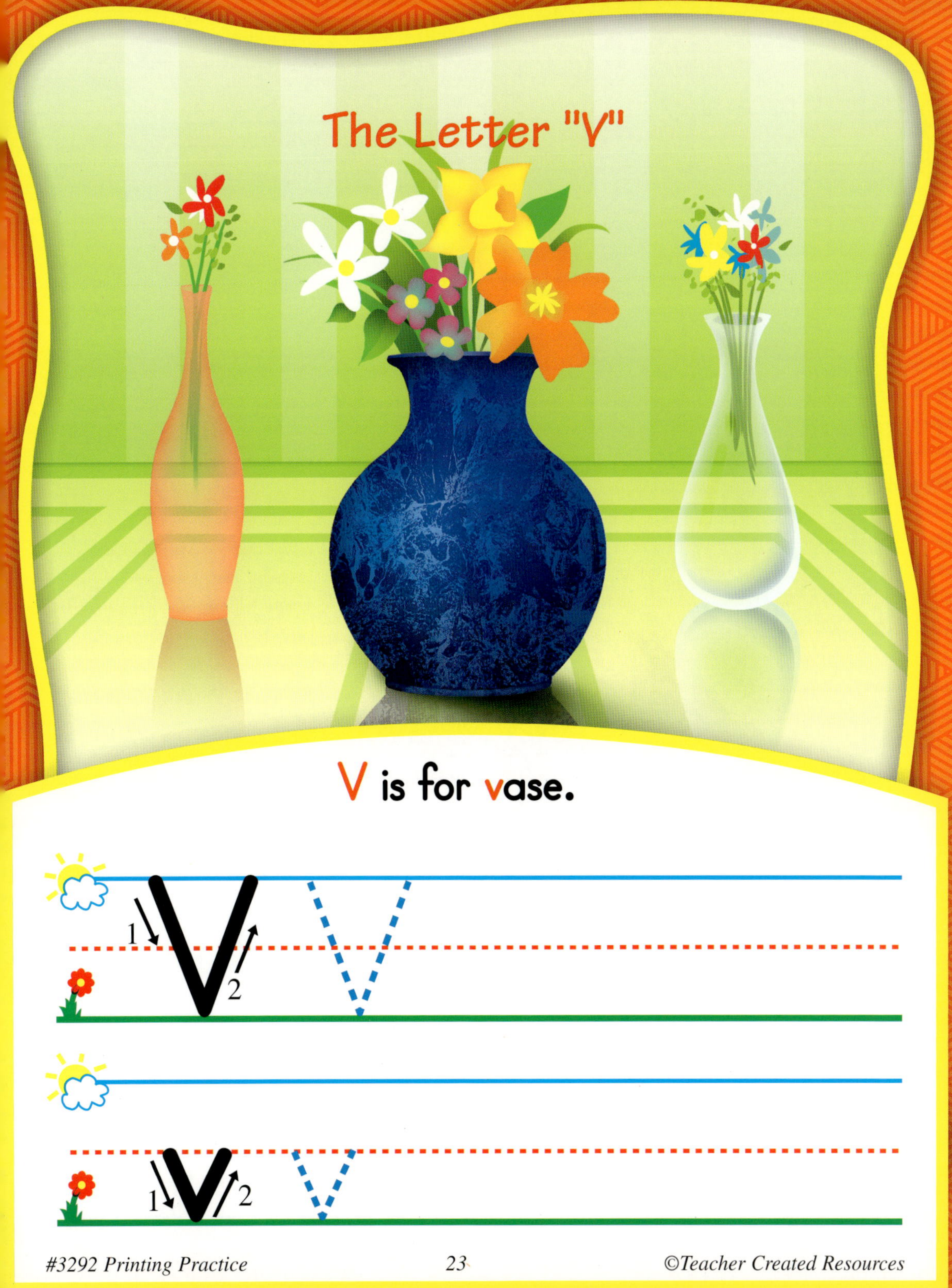

V is for **v**ase.

The Letter "W"

W is for wagon.

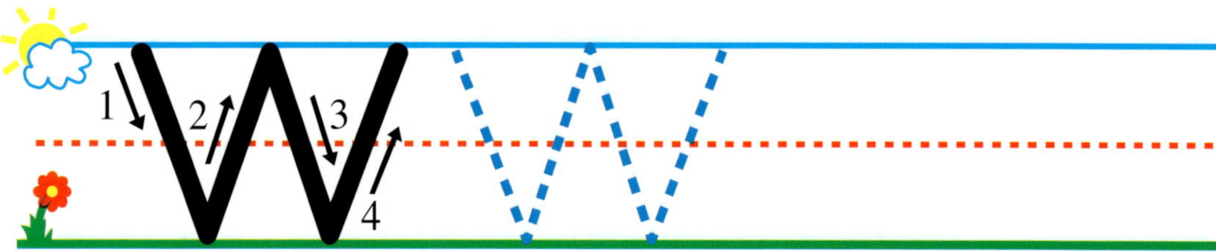

The Letter "X"

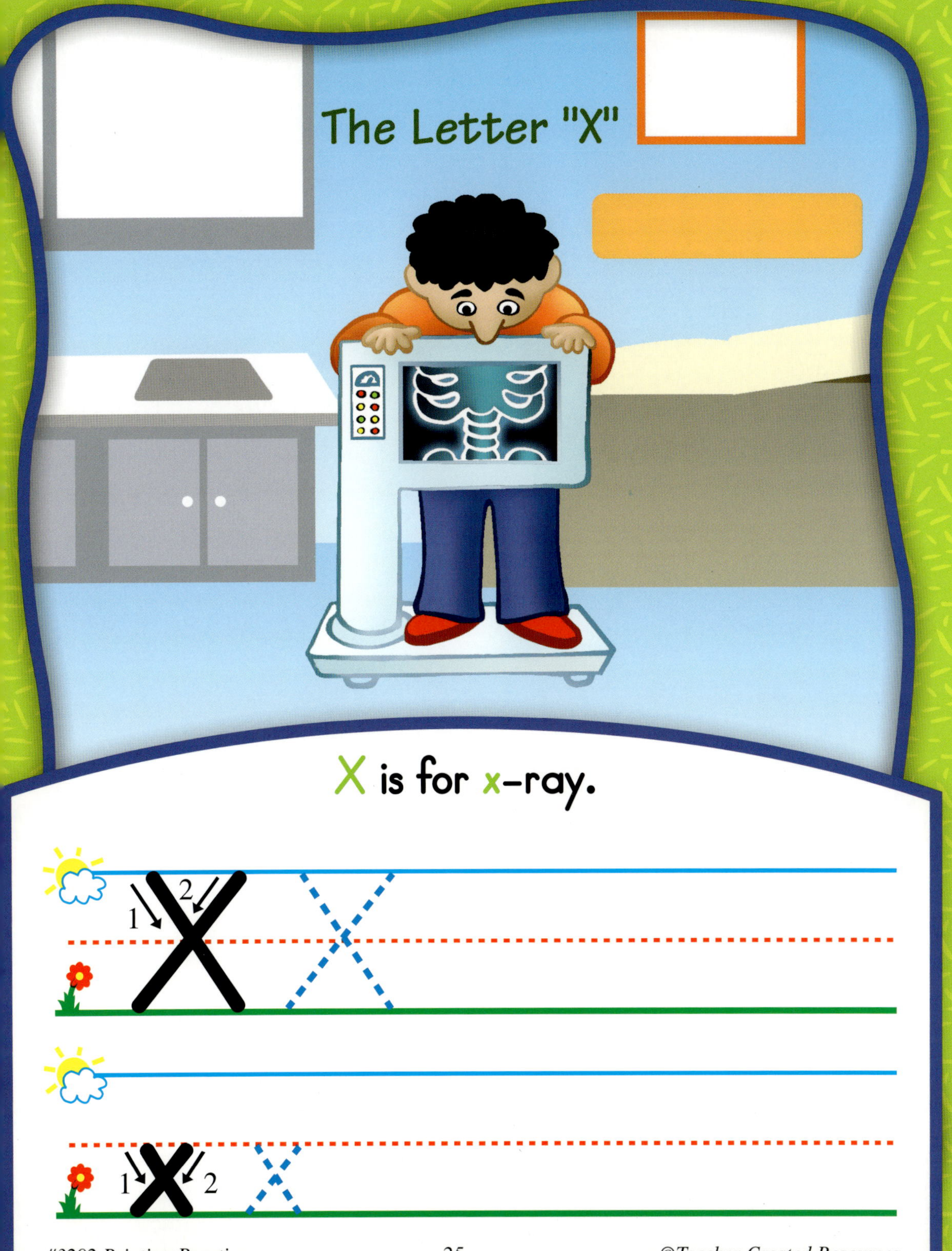

X is for x-ray.

The Letter "Y"

The Letter "Z"

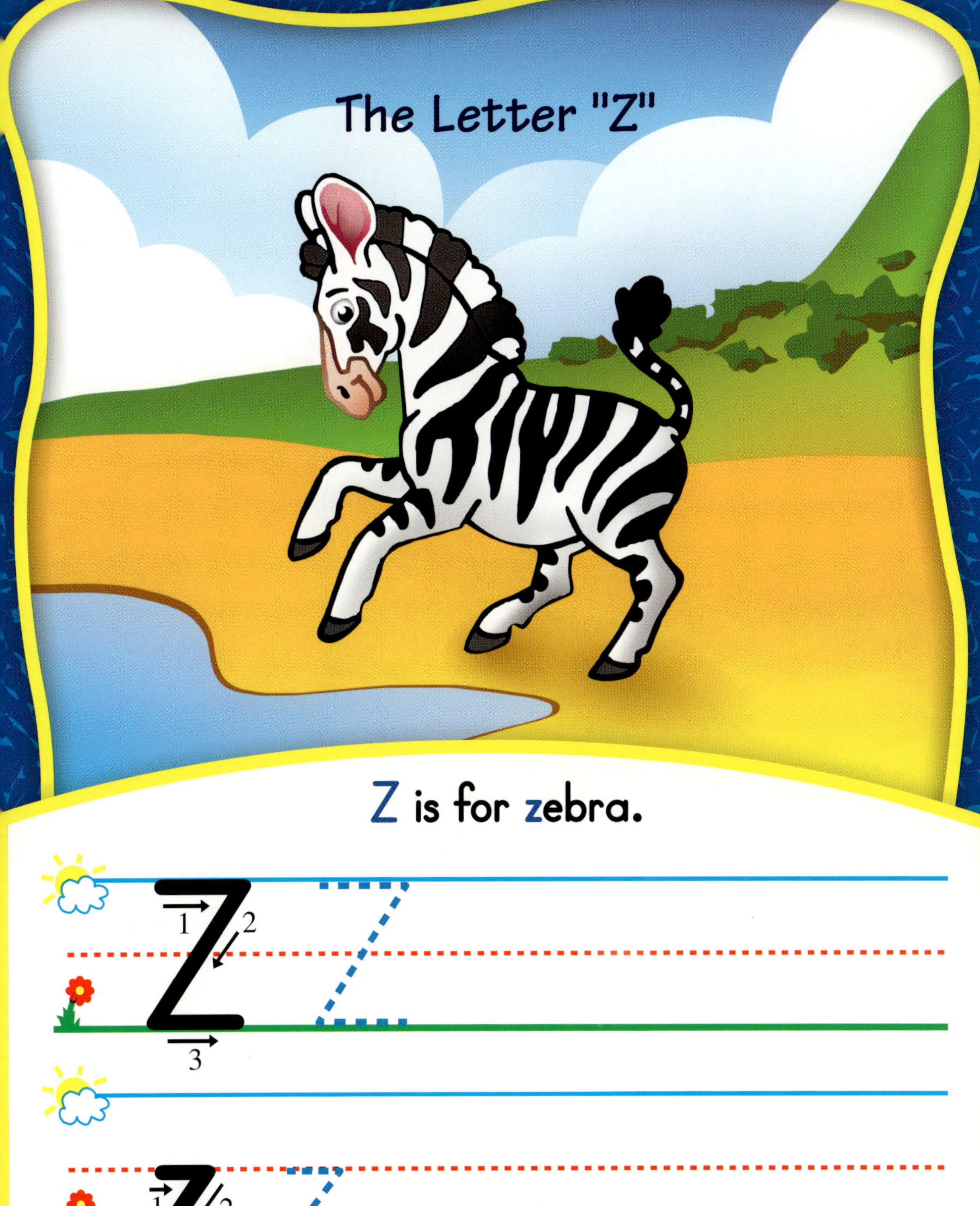

Z is for zebra.

What Comes Next?

Directions: Write the next letter in each series.

A B C D ___

R S T U ___

K L M N ___

G H I J ___

C D E F ___

V W X Y ___

P Q R S ___

I J K L ___

Under the Palm (A–Z)

Busy Bees (a–z)

Directions: Connect the dots from a to z. Start at the ★.
What did you draw?

Alphabet Maze

Baby Bear is hiding. Help Mama Bear follow the alphabet to find him.

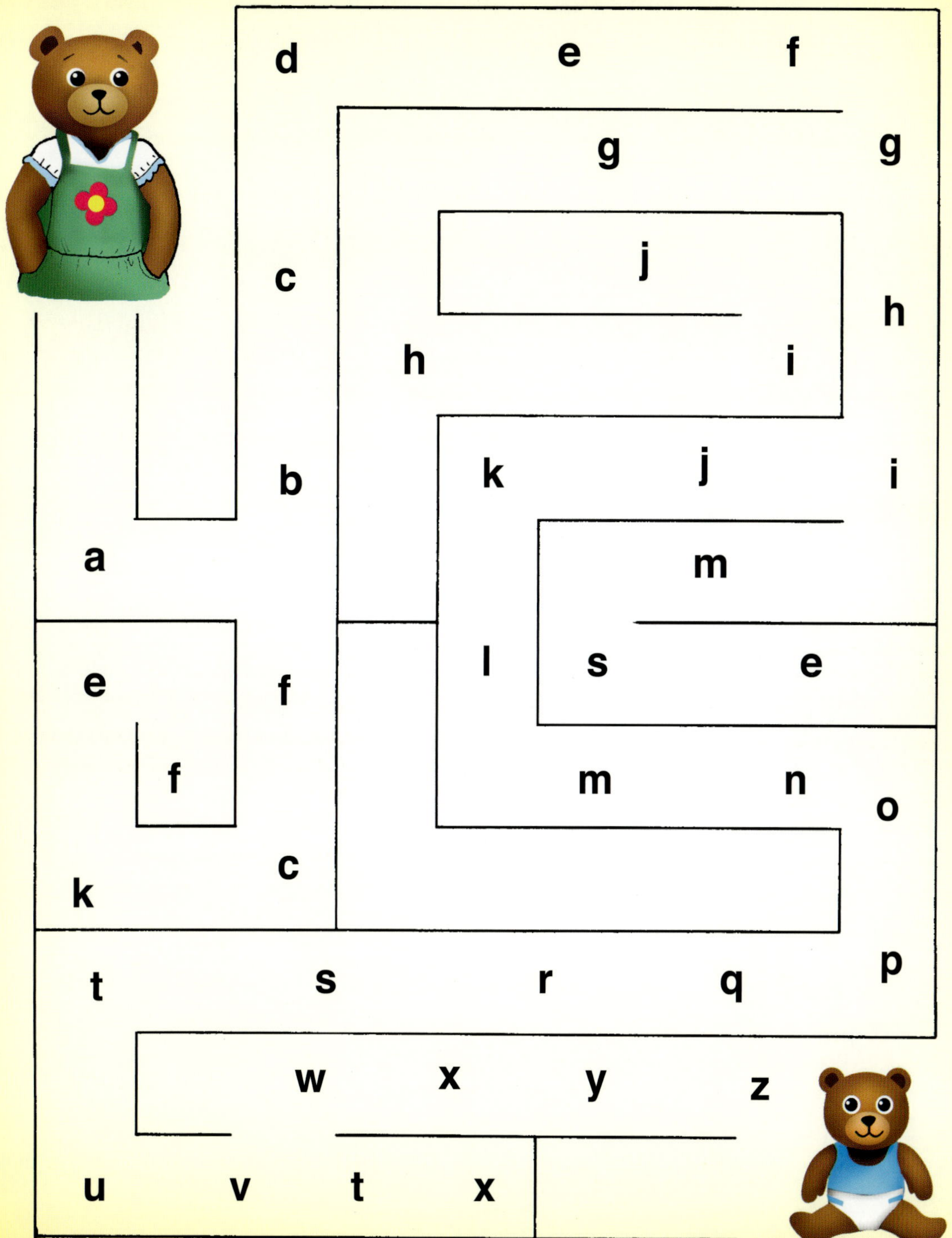

The Messy Room

Directions: Jason spilled his box of lowercase letters in his room. Help Jason find his lowercase letters. Circle the ones you find.